THE
SILK AND SPICE ROUTES

Exploration
by sea

STRUAN REID

UNESCO

🌷Belitha Press
UNESCO Publishing

UNESCO

Foreword

The story is told how Xiling Shi, while strolling one day in the garden, casually plucked a white cocoon from the leaf of a mulberry tree under which she was passing. She later chanced to drop the cocoon in a bowl of steaming tea and, in attempting to retrieve it, found herself unravelling a long white thread. Xiling Shi was the wife of Huangdi, the semi-mythical emperor who ruled China nearly 5000 years ago; and it was in this way, according to legend, that she discovered the secret of what was to become one of China's most valuable and distinctive products – silk.

Silk was in fact only one of many precious goods exchanged between East and West along what later came to be known as the Silk Roads. Jade and lapis lazuli were carried along these routes, as were spices, fruits and flowers such as ginger, pomegranates and roses. Some of our basic technologies like printing and paper-making were also transmitted along these ancient arteries. Ambassadors, scholars, craftsmen, entertainers, monks, pilgrims and soldiers all journeyed along the Silk Roads, acquiring and spreading knowledge as they went.

UNESCO is the United Nations agency responsible for promoting co-operation and understanding among nations in the areas of education, science, culture and communication. One of its current projects is the 'Integral Study of the Silk Roads: Roads of Dialogue', which seeks to explore and highlight the rich cultural exchanges and contacts that took place along the ancient Silk Roads. As part of this project, UNESCO has organized a series of expeditions over land and sea, retracing with international teams of scholars, film-makers, photographers and writers the journeys of those who travelled these routes down the ages.

I am sure you will enjoy reading this book in 'The Silk and Spice Routes' series, co-published by UNESCO and Belitha Press. I hope that your new knowledge about these fascinating channels of trade and communication will enable you to understand better some aspects of cultures different from your own. You will in this way – as unwittingly as Xiling Shi when she discovered silk – be adding your own personal thread to that precious web of understanding between members of the human family on which the future of our planet depends.

Federico Mayor
The Director-General
UNESCO

Contents

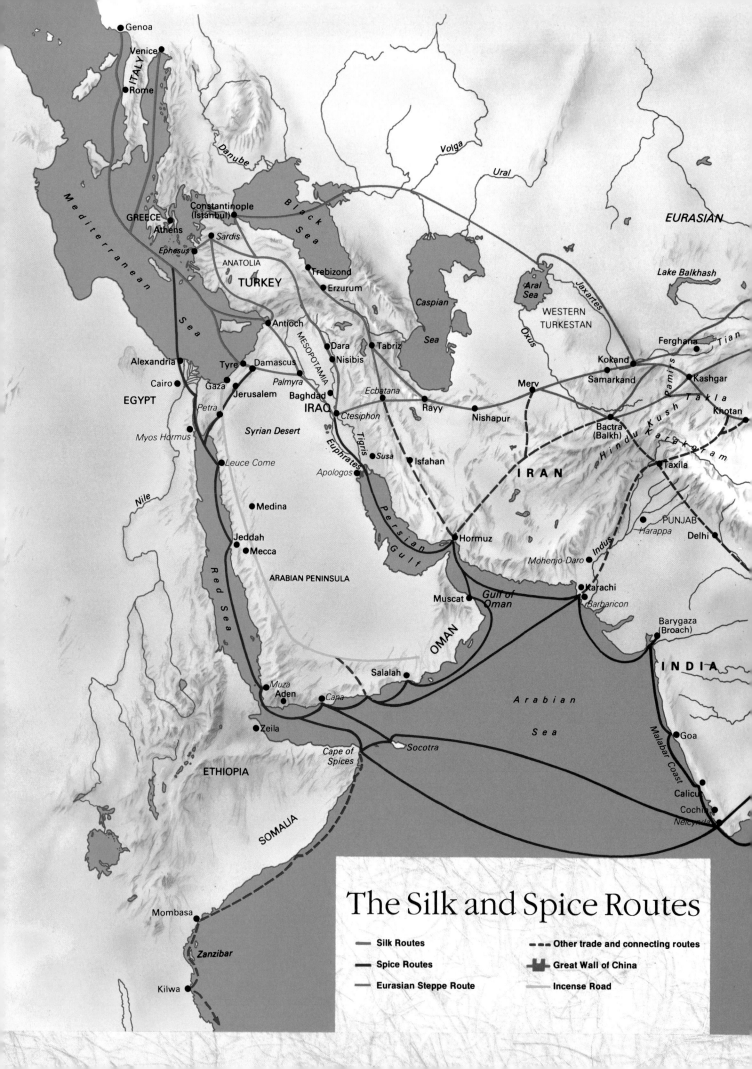

Genoa
Venice
ITALY
Rome
Danube
Mediterranean
Sea
Nile
Red Sea
EGYPT
Cairo
Alexandria
Myos Hormus
Leuce Come
Medina
Jeddah
Mecca
ARABIAN PENINSULA
Muza
Aden
Zeila
Cape of Spices
ETHIOPIA
SOMALIA
Mombasa
Zanzibar
Kilwa

GREECE
Athens
Ephesus
Sardis
ANATOLIA
TURKEY
Constantinople
(Istanbul)
Black Sea
Trebizond
Erzurum
Antioch
Tyre
Damascus
MESOPOTAMIA
Palmyra
Gaza
Jerusalem
Petra
Baghdad
IRAQ
Ctesiphon
Dara
Nisibis
Tabriz
Ecbatana
Rayy
Euphrates
Tigris
Susa
Apologos
Isfahan
Syrian Desert
Persian Gulf
Hormuz
Muscat
Gulf of Oman
OMAN
Salalah
Cana
Socotra
Arabian Sea

Caspian Sea
Aral Sea
Volga
Ural
WESTERN TURKESTAN
Oxus
Jaxartes
EURASIAN
Lake Balkhash
Merv
Nishapur
Kokand
Samarkand
Bactra (Balkh)
IRAN
Hindu Kush
Karakoram
Pamirs
Ferghana
Tian
Kashgar
Takla
Khotan
Taxila
PUNJAB
Harappa
Delhi
Mohenjo-Daro
Indus
Karachi
Barbaricon
Barygaza (Broach)
INDIA
Malabar Coast
Goa
Calicut
Cochin
Nelcynda

The Silk and Spice Routes

—— Silk Routes	- - - Other trade and connecting routes
—— Spice Routes	▆▆ Great Wall of China
—— Eurasian Steppe Route	—— Incense Road

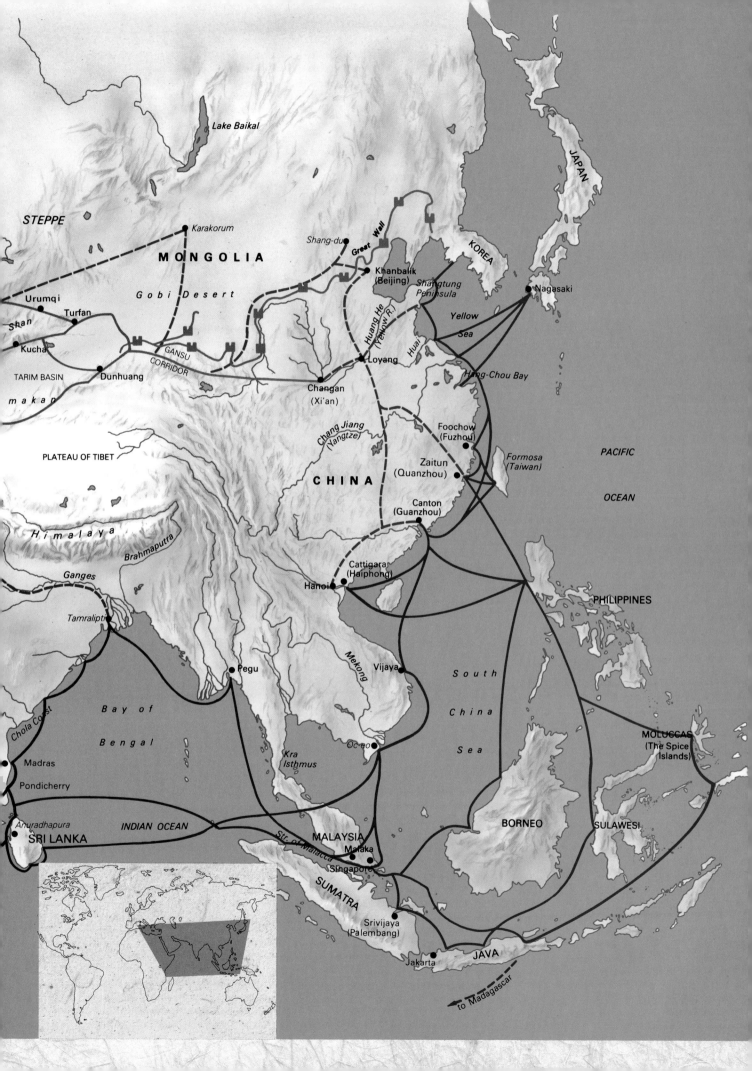

▲ *An 11th Century CE Chinese pottery incense burner.*

▼ *The busy Spice Route port of Antioch in the 15th Century CE.*

What are the Spice Routes?

The Spice Routes is the name given to the network of sea routes that link the East with the West. They stretch from the west coast of Japan, through the islands of Indonesia, around India to the lands of the Middle East – and from there, across the Mediterranean to Europe. It is a distance over 15,000 kilometres and, even today, is no easy journey.

From our very earliest history, people have travelled the Spice Routes. At first, they probably ventured only short distances from their home ports but over the centuries their ships sailed further and further across the oceans. They braved treacherous seas and a possibly hostile reception on arrival in an unknown land. These journeys were not undertaken purely in the spirit of adventure – the driving force behind them was trade. The Spice Routes were, and still are, first and foremost trade routes.

Trade is a central part of our lives. When we buy something we are trading, exchanging one item (usually money) for another. However, our purchase is the final link in a long chain of buyers and sellers: from the supplier of raw materials, to the manufacturer, to the wholesaler, to the shop – and if the goods we buy come from abroad there may be several other stages in between. The journey of the goods between all these links in the chain is called a trade route (in fact, the word 'trade' derives from a term meaning a track or course). In the case of the Spice Routes the links were formed by traders buying and selling goods from port to port. The principal and most profitable goods they traded in were spices – giving the routes their name. As early as 2000 BCE, spices such as cinnamon from Sri Lanka and cassia from China found their way along the Spice Routes to the Middle East. Other goods exchanged hands too – cargoes of ivory, silk, porcelain, metals and dazzling gemstones brought great profits to the traders who were prepared to risk the dangerous sea journeys.

But precious goods were not the only thing to be exchanged by the traders. Perhaps more important was the exchange of knowledge: knowledge of new peoples and their religions, languages, artistic and scientific skills. The ports along the Spice Routes acted as melting pots for ideas and information. With every ship that swept out with a cargo of valuables on board, fresh knowledge was carried over the seas to the ship's next port of call.

▲ Carving marble Buddhas in Burma. Ideas on religion spread along the Spice Routes.

▼ Colourful spices are still sold in the East today, just as they were thousands of years ago.

The Demand for Spices

Today, it seems strange that the demand for spices should be one of the central causes for such large scale trade across such massive distances. We probably think of them simply as a flavouring for food. Yet, the word 'spice' comes from the Latin *species*, which means an item of special value, as compared to ordinary articles of trade.

The great distances are easy to explain: many of the important spices grew only in the tropical East, from China south to Indonesia, southern India and Sri Lanka. In particular, they grew in the Moluccas or, as they are better known, the Spice Islands. These are a chain of mountainous islands strung out like jewels in the Pacific Ocean between Sulawesi (Celebes) and New Guinea. From here came the fragrant spices of cloves and nutmeg which grew nowhere else in the world. To reach the spice markets found across Asia and Europe, the spices *had* to be transported thousands of kilometres over the seas.

▲▶ *The two creatures shown on these pages are phoenixes from a Chinese silk tapestry of the 16th Century CE. The phoenix was a fantastic bird of ancient legend closely associated with the burning of incense. People believed that it burned itself in a fire and that another phoenix rose from its ashes.*

▶ *Spices have been used in the preparation and flavouring of food for thousands of years. Many of the great cuisines of the world have developed through the use of spices.*

How people came to know and value these spices which grew so far away is an impossible question to answer exactly. As trading links from Indonesia fanned out through south and central Asia, so they met with links that spread from the Middle East and the north. Goods were exchanged and traders would return to their homeland carrying the beautifully scented, exotic spices. Perhaps it was their strangeness and rarity that led great medicinal and spiritual values to be attributed to them.

From the dawn of civilization, spices were burned as incense in religious ceremonies, purifying the air and carrying the prayers of the people heavenward to their gods. They were also added to healing ointments and to potions drunk as antidotes to poisons. To hide the many household smells, people burned spices daily in their homes. They were used as cooking ingredients very early on – not only to add flavour but also to make the food, which was often far from fresh, palatable, particularly in hot climates.

Myths and legends were woven around these exotic substances. They were linked to strange beasts like the phoenix, giant eagles, serpents and dragons. In the Fifth Century BCE, the Greek historian Herodotus wrote how the spice cassia grew in a lake 'infested by winged creatures like bats, which screech alarmingly and are very pugnacious'. Some of these stories were probably created by the traders who, wishing to protect their profits, tried to hide the sources of the spices.

For the profits to be made from spices were huge. Because they were so small and dried, they were easy to transport, but they were literally worth their weight in gold. The wealth of the spice trade brought great power and influence and, over the centuries, bloody battles were fought to win control of it and the routes along which it took place.

▲ *Early 19th Century* CE *English spice boxes. Spices were extremely expensive and carefully stored in special boxes and cupboards.*

The Different Spices

A spice is the strongly flavoured dried flower, fruit, seed, bark or stem of a plant. For example, cloves are the unopened flower buds of the clove tree; nutmeg is a seed; cinnamon and cassia are bark; ginger and turmeric are both underground stems. In the past, as well as being used in food, spices were included in the ingredients of oils, ointments, perfume-powders, cosmetics, incense and medicine. Fragrant woods, such as sandalwood and aloe-wood, were also much in demand. Some of the most precious and sought-after spices carried along the Spice Routes are listed here.

Cloves *(Eugenia aromatica)* ▲

The clove tree is indigenous to the Moluccas of Indonesia. Today, they are also grown successfully elsewhere such as Madagascar and Grenada. Cloves are the dried flower-buds of the tree. They are used in curing meats, cooking and medicine.

Ginger *(Zingiber officinale)* ▲

This spice is the rhizome (an underground stem) of the ginger plant. It is used in food and medicines. The ginger plant originally grew in Java, India and China but is now farmed elsewhere as well. **Turmeric *(Curcuma longa)*** is a plant of the ginger family, native to India and Indonesia. Oil from its rhizomes was used in food and as a bright yellow dye.

▲
Nutmeg and Mace *(Myristica fragrans)*

The evergreen nutmeg tree is native to the tiny volcanic Banda Islands at the southern tip of the Moluccas. Now it is also grown in the West Indies, Sri Lanka and Malaysia. Inside the fruit, the heavy seed, the nutmeg, is covered by a scarlet lace-like mesh, the mace. Both were used in medicines and as an incense and, as is still the case today, in cooking.

Frankincense *(Boswellia sacra)* ▲

This is the resin of the frankincense tree. It was considered the highest quality incense. It was gathered from trees grown in the Zufar (Dhofar) region in the south of the Arabian Peninsula and in Somalia in Africa. **Myrrh *(Commiphora myrrha)*** is a fragrant resin from a shrub mostly grown in Somalia. Valued as highly as frankincense, myrrh was used as incense and as an ointment.

Camphor *(Dryobalanops aromatica & Cinnamomum camphora)* ▲

Camphor is sometimes called gum arabic. It is a strong-smelling crystalline substance obtained from the sap of two types of tree found in parts of the Far East. It was used mainly in incense and medicine.

Black pepper *(Piper nigrum)* ▼

One of the earliest spices known. It was once so valuable that it was often used as a substitute for money, ransoms, tributes and rents. The pepper plant is a climbing vine, with berries called peppercorns. It grows wild in the equatorial forests of India and Asia but is now cultivated. For many centuries, the best quality pepper has been grown on the western Malabar coast of India.

▲
Cinnamon and Cassia *(Cinnamomum macrophyllum & Cinnamomum cassia)*

These spices are two of the earliest known. Both were used to flavour food and in embalming ointments. They are the dried bark of the cinnamon and cassia trees – the first being native to Sri Lanka, the second to China and Burma, but now both are grown successfully elsewhere.

Saffron *(Crocus sativus)* ▲

Saffron is now the most expensive spice in the world. It is made from the stigmas (the pollen stalks) inside the saffron crocus flowers. Thousands of stigmas are needed for just a few grams. It can be used in foods, wines, perfumes and as a dye or a drug. It was grown mainly in Iran and India, but also now in Spain.

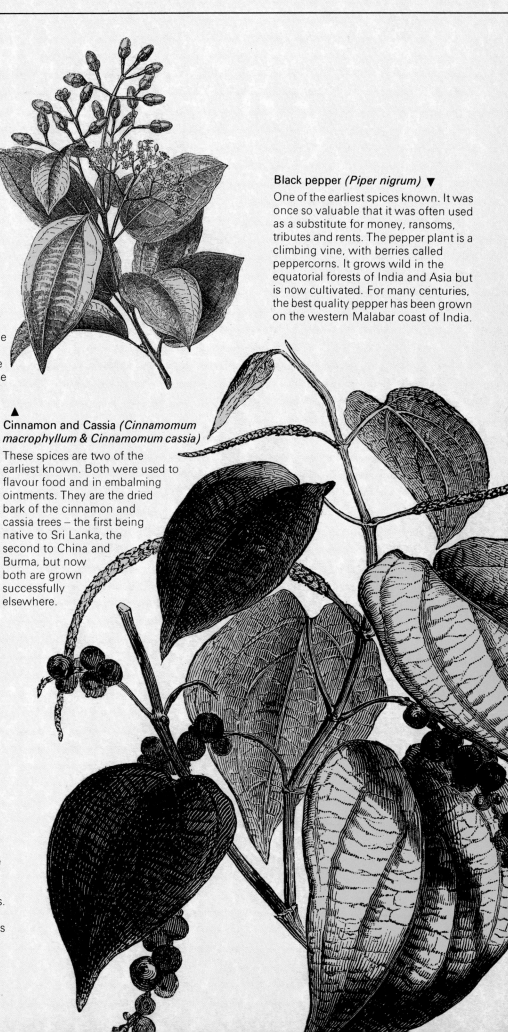

chapter two

Sailing East to West

From
China and Korea

▲ *A Chinese gold dagger handle of the 4th Century BCE. The Chinese were extremely skilled craftsmen, as shown in this elaborate workmanship.*

▶ *A Chinese cargo boat.*

▼ *A bronze rhinoceros, made in China in the late 3rd Century BCE. The rhinoceros was prized for its horns, which were used in medicines.*

Trade along the Spice Routes was at first fairly localized. It was not until around the Seventh and Eighth centuries CE that ships began to travel from China all the way to the Middle East and vice versa. But these longer voyages still followed routes that had been established centuries before.

In 1207 BCE, a ruling family came to power in northern China called the Zhou. Their dynasty, as such royal families were called in China, lasted for over 800 years until 221 BCE. During this time, the area of Chinese influence was extended and there was a great increase in trade with other nations. This expansion continued under the Han (202 BCE-220 CE), one of the greatest of the Chinese dynasties.

The ancient Chinese culture had produced superb craftsmen and their goods were greatly prized, in particular the beautiful material silk, which no other country knew how to make. Other exports included spices, such as cassia and ginger, iron and jade. Merchants from Korea, Japan and Southeast Asia congregated in the Chinese ports, exchanging their goods for those of the Celestial Empire.

One of the main peoples to trade with China were the Koreans. They traded both by land and sea. From 140 BCE, regular trade fairs were held on the northern Chinese frontier where furs and other valuable merchandise from the Korean Peninsula could be bought. Korean ships coasted round the northern edge of the Yellow Sea and made port on the Shantung Peninsula, whilst others crossed the open sea to Nagasaki in Japan. From here, they headed back again to China, making for the Huai or Yangtze Rivers or even for Hang-Chou Bay.

Further south, Chinese ships – their junks – carried cargoes round the coast to P'anyu (Canton) and Cattigara in North Vietnam. At this time, trade relations also existed between China and Java. Ships left Cattigara and Foochow further north and travelled via the Philippines to the Moluccas and East Java. The journey took several months in all but the ships returned laden with cargoes of cloves, nutmeg and mace.

From at least 200 BCE, Chinese junks sailed as far south as the Malay Peninsula and the Straits of Malacca. Here they met and traded not only with Indonesian peoples but also Indian merchants. For beyond the Straits lay the vast expanse of the Indian Ocean – and the wealth of India itself.

▲ Map showing the trade routes between China and Southeast Asia.

▼ A Chinese port crowded with junks bringing goods from around the world.

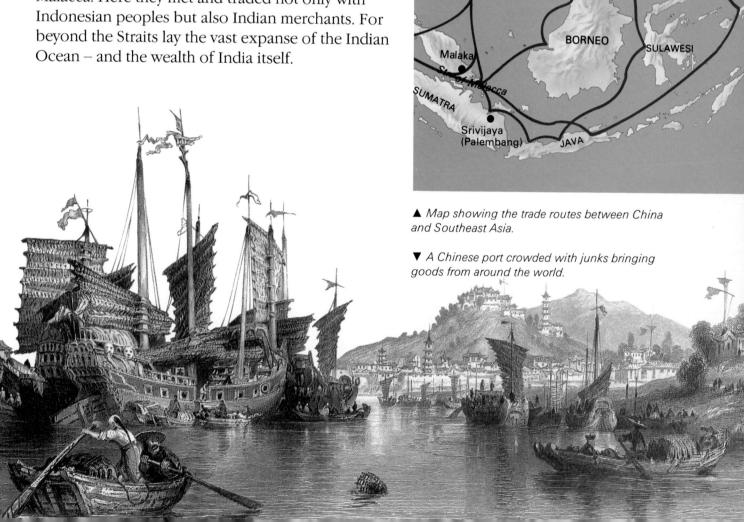

'Where the two monsoons meet'

▲ *The ruins of the Buddhist temple in Sri Lanka built by a king of Anuradhapura.*

▼ *Map outlining the trade routes from Southeast Asia to India.*

Lying at the junction between the Indian Ocean and the China Seas, the Malay Peninsula and the Indonesian Archipelago have always played a vital part in the trade between East and West. As the Portuguese observer Tomé Pires described it in the Sixteenth Century, it is 'where the two monsoons meet' – that is the monsoon winds of the Indian Ocean that blow from the south-west from April to October and from the north-east from October to April, and the trade winds of the China Seas. Ships from India could sail before the south-west monsoon in April and return home on the north-east wind in October. Similarly, ships from the ports of P'anyu and Cattigara sailed for the Indonesian ports in late autumn.

There were various different routes around the Malay Peninsula. Most trade was carried through the Straits of Malacca and whoever controlled this narrow stretch of water held the key to the spice trade. It lies between the tip of the Malay Peninsula and Sumatra. Cities overlooking the Straits, such as Srivijaya (near the site of modern-day Palembang) and, much later, Malaka, became rich and powerful. They would levy taxes on the ships that travelled back and forth on the Spice Route and, of course, were active in the trade themselves.

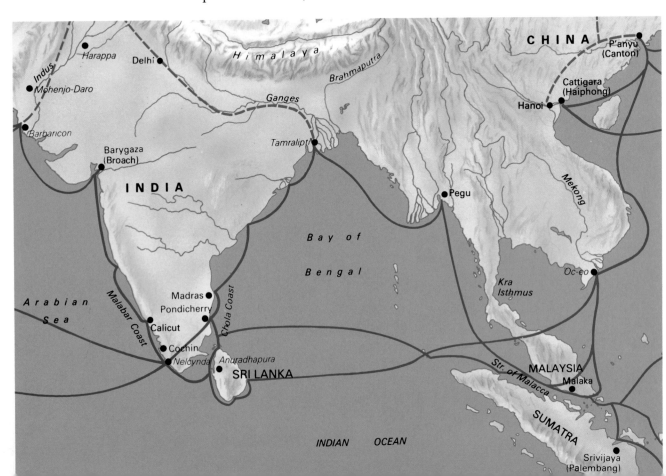

Another important trading centre was the port of Oc-eo on the Mekong Delta. Here Indian, Chinese and, later, western traders met to exchange their wares. Merchants travelling westwards might then return through the Straits but another route was used that crossed the Gulf of Siam to the Kra Isthmus. The precious cargoes were then transported by land over the peninsula to the Bay of Bengal, and loaded again on to Indian ships. Another similar crossing was made further south. These last two routes were often favoured as they avoided the more dangerous voyage around Tumasik (modern Singapore) where ruthless 'sea gypsies' or pirates were known to lurk.

From the Malay Peninsula, Sumatra and Java, ships sailed across the Indian Ocean heading for ports on the eastern Chola Coast of India. Others made their way to Sri Lanka, 'the Island of Rubies'. The trade helped establish wealthy kingdoms in this area. One such was the Anuradhapura kingdom of Sri Lanka that flourished from about 200BCE – its cities were full of parks, palaces and Buddhist temples. Their wealth came partly from trade – in cinnamon, ebony and Sri Lanka's famous rubies.

India was another important meeting point on the Spice Routes. From the Chola Coast of India and Sri Lanka, goods from the East were transported westwards by land and sea to the ports on the western Malabar Coast, such as Nelcynda, and further north Barygaza and Barbaricon. Here, once again, goods and money changed hands with the arrival of ships from the Middle East.

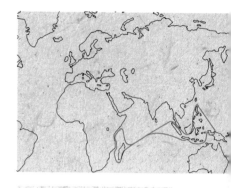

The Cinnamon Route
This was one of the most remarkable journeys of all time. It was a direct sea voyage from Southeast Asia to Madagascar off the east coast of Africa. From as early as 2000 BCE, Indonesian sailors in ocean-going canoes carried cinnamon, fragrant woods and other spices. Using the trade winds and ocean currents from the Indonesian Archipelago to Madagascar and East Africa, they travelled distances of over 6,000 kilometres.

◄ *An 18th Century engraving showing a ship passing through the Straits of Malacca.*

▼ *Some of the gold ceremonial jewellery of a Sri Lankan prince. Sri Lanka grew rich from trade.*

From India to Europe

Cargo ships of the ancient Egyptians are shown on this page. A very early record of Spice Route trade tells of Queen Hatshepsut (1490-1468 BCE) of Egypt sending ships to the land of Punt (probably in East Africa) to collect myrrh trees.

Like those between India and Southeast Asia, the paths of the Spice Routes between India and the Middle East were partly dictated by the monsoon winds. This meant that ships could sail direct from the Malabar Coast to Africa and the mouth of the Red Sea. However, from very early on routes also existed that followed the western coast of India north round to the Persian Gulf and the Arabian Peninsula.

Regular trade had taken place between the cities of Mohenjo-daro and Harappa in the River Indus valley and Mesopotamia since at least 2000 BCE.

By 200 BCE, trade was on a far greater scale and along several different routes. Cotton cloth from eastern India and perfumed oils were traded from the west coast ports of India for cherry-red coral from the Mediterranean and amber from the Baltic, along with the spices that were produced all around the Indian Ocean. India and the Middle East, particularly southern Arabia, were both production and collection centres. Both regions produced important spices and other trade goods and both, by virtue of their geographical location, acted as meeting and distribution points of the different routes.

The Periplus of the Erythraeum Sea is a document written in around 80 CE believed to be by a Greek sea captain based in Alexandria. It gives a good picture of the Spice Routes of this time. From Barbaricon, ships could take a northerly route to Hormuz at the entrance to the Persian Gulf and on up to Apologos. From here, the cargoes joined the land routes from Ctesiphon and the East to travel overland via the Tigris and Euphrates valleys to the splendid cities of Petra (now in Jordan) and Palmyra (in Syria) – cities built with the wealth generated by trade. From these crossroads of the various overland trade routes, goods were redistributed and carried on to the ports of Gaza, Tyre and Antioch on the eastern Mediterranean and so on to Europe.

From Barygaza and the Malabar ports, ships took the more southerly route across the Arabian Sea. They sailed via the island of

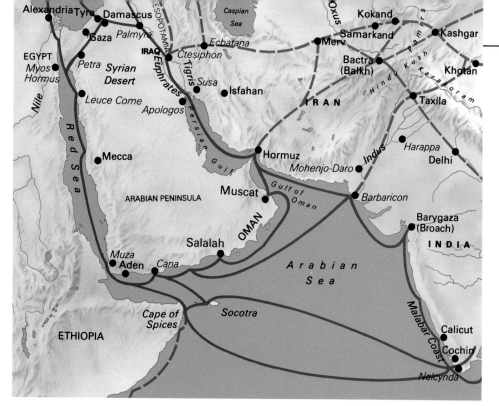

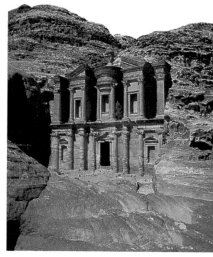

Socotra, the 'Isle of the Blest' – a major crosssroads of the sea trade lying off the Cape of Spices (now Cape Gardafui) – and then on to Cana or later Salalah on the coast of the Arabian Peninsula. From here, cargoes were taken up the Red Sea, the route dividing after Leuce Come, when travellers could continue up through Palestine to Petra or cross the sea to Egypt and the great port of Alexandria.

Over the centuries the routes described here were to vary slightly. As cities and kingdoms flourished, trade would flow through them, but if their power dwindled so too would the trade as merchants found safer routes to follow and wealthier markets to sell to. But, partly through geographical necessity, the main links in the Spice Routes were laid down early in their history.

◀ *Map of the sea routes from India to the Middle East and Mediterranean.*

▲ *View of el-Deir (the Monastery) at Petra, Jordan. Petra lay at the crossroads of many trade routes, and its people, the Nabataeans, grew rich from taxing the goods that passed through their lands.*

▼ *A 15th Century French illustration showing the pepper harvest on the Malabar Coast of western India. Its pepper crop made the Malabar Coast an important port of call for Spice Route traders.*

chapter three

Expanding Empires – Expanding Trade

The Legacy of Alexander

▲ *This Roman mosaic is based on a Greek painting from the time of Alexander. It depicts the Battle of Issos (333 BCE) between Alexander (shown left) and King Darius of Persia (centre).*

▼ *A Greek merchant ship painted on a cup dating from 540 BCE.*

The first millennium before the Common Era saw a great increase in maritime trade around the Mediterranean. This was largely handled by two great seafaring peoples – the Greeks and the Phœnicians. By establishing a network of trading colonies, both dominated large areas of the Mediterranean coastline. In their hands, goods from the East that reached the Mediterranean along the Spice Routes were transported still further west.

However, the ancient Persian Empire (established around 550 BCE) and smaller kingdoms of the Middle East maintained an effective grip on the east-west trade with India and beyond. But, in the Fourth Century BCE, a Greek leader emerged who was to change this. His name was Alexander the Great.

Born in 356 BCE, Alexander became ruler of Macedonia in northern Greece in 336 after the death of his father, Philip. Having swiftly consolidated his father's campaign to control the whole of

Greece, he turned his attention eastwards. The wealth of the trading kingdoms of the Middle East, and in particular the Persian Empire, was more than enough temptation for the ambitious leader. In 334 BCE, Alexander and his armies crossed into Asia to fight a campaign whose successes have passed into legend. By the time of his death in 323 BCE, he had established a Greek empire that stretched from Egypt across Asia to the River Indus of northern India. He was not quite 33 years old.

As Alexander conquered, he also colonized, founding new cities which he populated not only with local peoples but also with Greek administrators, craftsmen and merchants. The Greeks, already experienced international traders, were keen to exploit the possibilities of their new markets and new sources of supply. The city of Alexandria in Egypt, founded by Alexander at the mouth of the River Nile, was to be one of the major distribution and refinement points of Spice Routes trade for several centuries to come. In addition, Greek sailors now had access to the Red Sea and Persian Gulf and so to the west coast ports of India.

After his death, Alexander's empire fragmented but was still largely Greek controlled. The Greek language, philosophy and ideas spread throughout western Asia, while Greek knowledge of the world beyond Europe was vastly increased. Amongst other things came new information on plants and their products, including spices, which formed the basis for Greco-Roman medicine and cosmetics and food flavouring. Theophrastus (372-288 BCE), sometimes known as 'the father of botany', wrote at this time. He was the first person to describe all known plants by categories, list their uses and where they came from.

All this knowledge was to be inherited and expanded upon by the next European power to attempt to control the trade routes through the Middle East – the Romans.

▲ *Alexander's empire in 323 BCE.*

▼ *A page from a book called* De Materia Medica *written by Dioskorides, a Roman army physician, in 65 CE. Nearly all the prescriptions contained in the book include at least one spice from Arabia, the Far East or Africa. The tradition for books of this nature dates back to Theophrastus.*

The Romans' Quest for Spices

▲ *Augustus (63 BCE-14 CE), first Roman emperor.*

The Incense Road

From about 1000 BCE, long winding camel caravans travelled 2,700 kilometres up the length of the Arabian Peninsula along a route that is known as the Incense Road. They carried frankincense and myrrh from southern Arabia (today's Yemen and Oman) to the markets of the north. Southern Arabia became so rich from this trade that the Romans called it *Arabia Felix* (Arabia the Fortunate). The path of the Incense Road is marked on the map below, which also shows the extent of the Roman Empire in 14CE.

Towards the end of the Third Century BCE, Rome emerged as the main rival to the Greeks in the Mediterranean. By 133 BCE, its territories included all of Italy, Greece itself, much of Spain and parts of North Africa and Turkey. The vast and ever-increasing empire generated huge wealth and the Roman citizens looked towards the East for luxuries on which to spend it.

However, Roman access to the trade from the East was limited. The goods reached them through a series of middlemen and, as a result, were exorbitantly priced. The Parthians, the successors to the Greeks in Persia, held a strong grip on many of the land routes and access to the Spice Routes via the Persian Gulf. So it was to the Red Sea trade that the Romans turned their attentions.

In 30 BCE, Augustus, soon to become the first Roman emperor, made Egypt a Roman province. This was an important move as Egypt, with its port of Alexandria, was one of the main entry points for spices and other luxury goods into the Mediterranean. However, a group of states in southern Arabia (including today's Yemen and Oman) held the other end of the Red Sea route to India and also the Incense Road. Like the Parthians, they therefore controlled the trade that passed along them. Roman attempts to gain power over this by force failed dismally, and Augustus had to change his policy: he built large new ships and opened up a direct service between Egypt and India.

The early voyages by Roman ships were very dangerous and undertaken by less than 20 ships a year. The journey took two years to complete, the ships hugging the coastline and stopping at many ports along the way. But, by the reign of the Emperor Tiberius (14-37 CE), the Romans had learnt how to exploit the monsoon winds of the Indian Ocean – information first discovered by a Greek sailor, Hippalus, a century before. This completely changed the Roman use of the Spice Routes. Now they could sail direct from Cana to the Malabar Coast of India where the coveted black pepper grew.

Until then, spices had been extremely expensive. The new Spice Route bypassed so many of the middlemen and gave access to such plentiful supplies that the price of spices in the Empire dropped by more than half. Every April the Roman government sent a fleet of 120 large ships from Myos Hormus in the Red Sea to the Malabar Coast, which returned the following March. The whole journey took less than a year. Spices, silks and luxury goods from the East flowed into Europe as never before whilst, in exchange, the Romans sent metals, dyes, cloth, drugs and glassware to the expanding markets of Asia.

▲ *This Roman ivory plaque shows a priestess sprinkling frankincense on the altar of the god, Jupiter.*

Camel caravans still travel the deserts of North Africa and the Arabian Peninsula today.

The Chinese look
Westwards

▲ *A sacred Chinese Buddhist hanging painted on silk during the Tang Dynasty. The increase in China's foreign trade brought with it new ideas on religion and styles of art.*

If the Romans were looking to the East for their luxuries, so too the Chinese were looking increasingly beyond their borders to trade. At much the same time as Rome was emerging as the dominant power in Europe, China was entering an age of great prosperity and progress under the Han Dynasty.

In 221 BCE, the various kingdoms of China had been unified for the first time under the Qin Dynasty but they had been unable to maintain power after the death of the 'First Emperor', Zhang, in 210 BCE. Civil war ensued and it was the Han that emerged victorious in 202 BCE. As China's empire grew under the Han, so did her trade over land and sea.

It was during the reign of the Emperor Wu-di (140-86 BCE) that Chinese expansion resulted in the opening of a major trade route that linked East with West by land. Running through the heart of the Asian landmass, this was the famous Silk Route. Over the next 1600 years it was to be the main rival to the Spice Routes as a channel for international trade.

The Han had pushed into Central Asia to defend their territories from the northern barbarian tribe, the Xiongnu (later known in Europe as the Huns). In doing so, they discovered the huge markets for Chinese goods, such as silk and iron, in western Asia. The Chinese were equally delighted with the exotic items they received in return. Describing the imperial court of this period, the Han historian Pan Ku wrote: 'Precious articles like shining pearls, rhinoceros horns, tortoise shells and emeralds overflowed in the inner palace . . . In short, rare things of various places came from all directions.'

Han power dwindled during the Second Century CE. China fragmented but the trade the Han had built up continued on a limited scale along both the Silk and Spice Routes. When the Empire reunited

under the Sui Dynasty (580-618 CE), the trade links were there to be exploited on an even greater scale and to grow still further under the Tang (618-970 CE). By the Eighth Century, huge ships called at Canton laden with cargoes of spices, ivory, frankincense and other precious goods, making the port one of the greatest in the world.

Ships now came not only from Korea and Indonesia, but from Sri Lanka, India and even the Middle East. Chinese records of the time report that the largest ships came from Sri Lanka. They were 65 metres long and carried as many as 700 men. But, significantly, the most important ships were the 'Persian Argosies' – the ships of sailors who practised the new Muslim religion.

▲ ▲ *The Silk Route* (top) *passed through high mountains and across deserts. But it was political unrest and not the difficult terrain that would disrupt Silk Route trade. When this happened, the Spice Routes still provided a channel for east-west trade.*

▲ *This picture of a horse is taken from a stone relief in a Han Dynasty tomb in China.*

chapter four

The Arab Monopoly

The Empire of Islam

▲ *An illustration of Arab merchants on a trading mission. The Arabs were skilled sailors, their navigational skills perfected over many centuries of Spice Route trade.*

▼ *The blue area on this map shows the extent of Muslim power in 814.*

Early in the Seventh Century CE, the Prophet Muhammad preached the new religion of Islam to the Arabs of central and southern Arabia. On his death in 632 CE, he left an organized community of Muslims who were determined to carry his message to the world. The Muslim Arab armies swept through the Middle East. They captured the Egyptian port of Alexandria in 641 and by 710 their empire stretched from Spain to the Pamir mountains of Central Asia. Many of the peoples they conquered converted to Islam and from this religious unity developed an empire of great variety and dazzling grace. It was ruled by successive dynasties: the Umayyads, the Abassids, the Fatimids and the Turkish 'slave' dynasty of the Mamelukes.

Even before the rise of Islam, the Arabs had been active traders. Their share of the Red Sea trade had greatly increased with the decline of Roman power there in the Fourth Century CE and now the Spice Routes of the Persian Gulf came under their control as well. These had previously been in the hands of the Sasanians (224-651 CE), the successors to Parthian rule in Iran. Sasanian ships had sailed regularly to Sri Lanka and were already trading at Spice Route ports as far east as southern China. The Arabs now added their considerable sailing skills to these activities and Muslims came to dominate the Spice Route trade right across Asia and down the east coast of Africa. Much of the trade was direct to the source of supply so cutting out the expense of a middleman. Where they travelled and traded, the Muslims also converted, further consolidating their hold on the trade network from the East.

The monopoly of trade brought wealth and prosperity to the Middle East. There was a blossoming of literature and learning, founded on Arab intellectual and scientific traditions and those the Muslims inherited from the Sasanians and classical Europe. It was fed by the information brought back by Spice Route merchants. New knowledge of spices is reflected in the works of the Iranian doctor Ibn Sina (980-1037). His *Canon of Medicine,* which was to dominate medical teaching in Europe until the Seventeenth Century, includes details of the preparation of drugs from spices and herbs.

The skills of Muslim artisans were also enhanced by techniques learnt from abroad. Chinese weavers were brought to Iran, contributing to the growth of the silk industry there. The production of ceramics increased with the Muslims adopting many of the techniques used by the Tang Chinese and copying their decorative styles long after the Tang Dynasty had ended.

▲ *An illustration from a 12th Century Persian botanical treatise. It shows the tapping of balsam trees for their sap.*

▼ *A view of the interior of the Umayyad Mosque in Damascus, Syria.*

European Middlemen

▲ *The lion of St. Mark, patron saint of Venice.*

▼ *The Grand Canal in Venice. The city grew fabulously wealthy in her position as broker between Arabs and Europeans and beautiful palaces and churches were built beside the canals.*

Whilst Muslim commerce and culture flourished in the Middle East through the Seventh to Twelfth Centuries, the situation was very different in Christian Europe. The Roman Empire had slowly crumbled from the start of the Fourth Century and by 610 CE had lost all power in western Europe. Its remnants, the Byzantine Empire, was now focused on the City of Constantinople (today's Istanbul in Turkey). Constantinople continued many of the old traditions of Rome, while the taste for luxuries if anything increased. New trade routes sprang up around the city and, despite decreases in territory, the Empire's economy boomed.

Western Europe, however, sank into turmoil and the flow of goods reaching it from the East was reduced to a trickle. Trade on a large scale was not to revive until the Christian Crusades (1095-1291), which were launched to capture the holy city of Jerusalem from the Muslims. The crusaders saw what riches poured into the Muslim world from the East – spices and silks, porcelain and precious stones – and they developed a taste for the exotic foods, flavour and perfumes.

The Muslim barrier to western trade with the East was almost impassable but the Italian ports of Venice and Genoa exploited this situation. The merchants of these city-states made trade agreements with the Muslims and set themselves up as the main suppliers

◄ *A 15th Century French illustration of crusaders disembarking at the port of Damietta in Egypt, on their way to Jerusalem. They are being blessed by bishops as they leave the boat. The Crusades brought the riches of the East to the attention of Europe once again.*

▼ *The port and city of Genoa today.*

to the crusaders. Once they had reached the Mediterranean ports, the Oriental goods were sold by the Muslim traders to Venetian and Genoese merchants, who then resold them in Europe at exorbitant prices. The further these goods made their way into Europe, the more transactions had to be negotiated, with each transaction adding to the sale price. For example, a hundredweight of pepper cost only three ducats in the Indian port of Calicut, but the Venetians could sell it in Europe for eighty.

The two Italian cities grew enormously rich from their trading links with the Muslims. But a bitter rivalry grew up between them and also Constantinople. In 1204 the Venetians were chosen to lead the Fourth Crusade against Alexandria but instead attacked Constantinople. Venice grabbed the most profitable areas of the Byzantine Empire for itself along with its lucrative trade in pepper with Alexandria.

Still later, the rivalry between Venice and Genoa came to a head with the Chioggia War (1378-81) from which Venice emerged victorious. Now Venice reigned supreme: ships filled its harbours and merchants bargained for the spices, perfumes and silks of the East. Its arsenal was the most impressive in the Mediterranean and the palaces and squares lining its canals were some of the most splendid in Europe.

The Travels of
Ibn Battuta

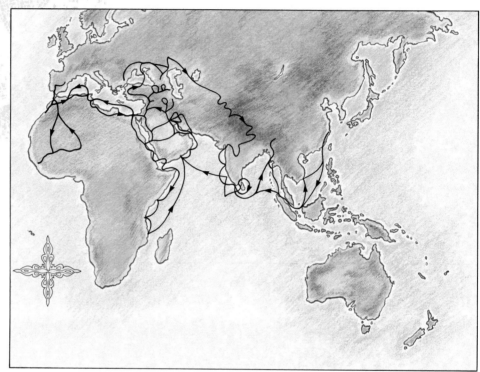

▲ *A Byzantine mosaic of Mary and the Infant Jesus, from a church in Istanbul. Ibn Battuta visited Constantinople, as it then was, and marvelled at its buildings.*

▶ *Map showing the complicated routes taken by Ibn Battuta on his travels.*

▼ *A view of Mecca, with the sacred Kaaba in the centre. Mecca was Ibn Battuta's original destination, but he continued his journeys for another 23 years.*

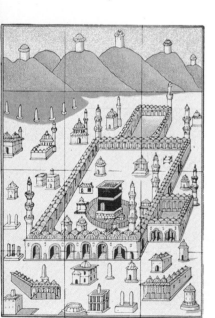

In 1325, a twenty-one year old Muslim called Ibn Battuta left his home in Tangier, Morocco to make the sacred pilgrimage to Mecca. It was the start of one of the greatest journeys of exploration made during the Medieval era.

It seems that on the way to Mecca, Ibn Battuta had gained a taste for travel for, rather than returning home, he went north to Baghdad. Over the next 23 years, he was to visit cities as far flung as Constantinople and Kilwa (on Africa's east coast); Calicut on the Malabar Coast of India and Canton in China. Still later, having returned briefly to Morocco, he visited Spain and even journeyed to Timbuktu in west Africa. He finally settled near Fez and, on the instructions of the Sultan of Morocco, wrote down the account of all his travels. He died in 1369.

Ibn Battuta travelled slowly, following no set plan and often staying in one place for years at a time. As a result, his account provides a vivid evocation of the world at this time and the network of trade routes that he followed. He describes many of the Spice Route ports and cities: Cairo was 'peerless in beauty and splendour' whilst Zaila in Somalia was 'the dirtiest town in the world'. The port of Calicut was 'visited by merchants from China, Sumatra, Sri Lanka, the Maldives, Yemen and Fars [Iran]' and the port of Zaitun (modern Quanzhou) in China was remarkable for its harbour. 'The harbour. . . is one of the greatest in the world – I am wrong: it is the *greatest!*' enthused Ibn Battuta.

The days of a unified empire of Islam were long since over and, by Ibn Battuta's time, much of Asia lay in the hands of the Mongols. A fierce warrior tribe from the north-east Steppes, the Mongols had swept through Asia, including most of China and Iran, crushing any opposition with immense brutality. Ibn Battuta describes how shocked he was to find Baghdad, once the great capital of the Abassid Dynasty (750-1258), in ruins, destroyed in 1258 by the Mongol onslaught. But now Mongol rule meant there was peace through Asia and travel was relatively safe. Ibn Battuta commented that in China, under the Mongol (Yuan) Dynasty (1264-1368), 'a man may go by himself on a nine-month journey, carrying with him large sums of money, without any fear'.

▲ *The ruins of Daulatabad (City of Fortune), the capital city of the Sultan of Delhi. Ibn Battuta worked there as a judge for 8 years.*

◄ *A Yuan Dynasty drawing of the rice harvest. Ibn Battuta was impressed by the order and security of Yuan ruled China.*

But although Muslim power had fragmented, the religion itself prospered, particularly along the Spice Routes. Ibn Battuta found practising Muslims as far east as Sumatra and through much of India. He describes several of the Muslim rulers he met: the Sultan of Sumatra was 'a humble-hearted man who walks on foot to Friday prayer', whereas the Sultan of Delhi was 'fondest of making gifts and shedding of blood'!

Ibn Battuta visited the lands of every Muslim ruler of the time – the only medieval traveller known to do this – as well as such 'infidel' countries as Byzantium, Sri Lanka and China. He set out only one year after the death of Marco Polo, the Venetian merchant whose journey to China is so famous. According to one calculation, Ibn Battuta's journeys covered a total distance of 120,700 kilometres – three times that travelled by Marco Polo.

▲ *A souk (market) in Fez, Morocco. Many of these markets look much as they did in Ibn Battuta's day.*

chapter five

A New Route East

Portuguese Exploration

▲ *Prince Henry of Portugal (1394-1460), known as the 'Navigator'.*

As the writings of Ibn Battuta reveal, the Spice Route Trade of the Fourteenth Century was still dominated by the Muslims. This control was to continue through much of the Fifteenth Century and, if anything, increase with the fall of Constantinople to the Muslim Turks in 1453.

Demand in Europe for exotic eastern goods was growing but the Europeans depended on Muslim merchants to supply them with these goods – a trade that was handled exclusively by Venice and Genoa. As other wealthy trading centres emerged in Europe, there was more and more resentment of the stranglehold the Muslims and the two Italian cities had over the markets. To bypass the middlemen, an alternative route to the East was needed.

It was the Portuguese who were the first to take up the challenge this presented. With their long Atlantic coastline, they were already experienced seafarers and, by early in the Fifteenth Century, were benefiting from the development of a new type of ship, the caravel. This was light but broad of beam and capable of carrying a good

supply of water and provisions. Exploration by sea was also actively encouraged by Prince Henry (1394-1460), the fourth son of King John I of Portugal and known as the 'Navigator'. Partly inspired by a Christian zeal to defeat the Muslims, from 1418 Henry began to send expeditions from Portugal to sail down the west coast of Africa.

At first they failed to progress beyond Cape Bojador, on the African coast near the Canary Islands. The sailors believed that beyond this point was 'the Green Sea of Darkness' where monsters lurked waiting to devour them. But in 1434, a captain called Gil Eannes persuaded his crew to sail beyond the dreaded cape. From then on other Portuguese expeditions ventured further and further south, trading with the local people and bringing back more information on the African coastline.

▲ *An engraving of a Portuguese caravel. These sturdy but nimble ships borrowed some of their design from the Arab boats called dhows.*

From about 1443, Henry resided at Sagres, on the most south-westerly point in Europe. Here he convened pilots and geographers who gathered together the information that accumulated from the African expeditions. Mapmakers could improve their charts and maps, encouraging still further exploration. By the time Prince Henry died in 1460, Portuguese ships had not yet travelled round the southern tip of Africa but the foundations had been laid for intrepid Portuguese sailors to achieve this, so reaching India and the riches of the East.

The Final Breakthrough

▲ This is a view of the Cape of Good Hope, the most southerly point in Africa, rounded by Bartolomeu Dias in 1488.

In 1481, John II succeeded as King of Portugal. He continued the work of his great-uncle Prince Henry, and in August 1487, an expedition under the command of Bartolomeu Dias set sail from Lisbon. This was finally to achieve the Portuguese aims. In a terrifying storm in February 1488 that lasted nearly two weeks, Dias and his crew were blown round the *Cabo Tormentoso* (the 'Stormy Cape', later renamed the Cape of Good Hope), the southernmost point of Africa.

Dias sailed a short way up the coast of Africa and then returned home. That a new route to the East had been found was confirmed by details of the Muslim trade networks that King John now received. These were sent by a Portuguese spy, Pedro da Covilha, who, disguised as an Arab trader, had travelled to the port of Sofala at the mouth of the Zambezi, only 2,000 kilometres north of the Cape.

John died in 1495 and it took his successor, King Manuel I, some time to find the backing for further expeditions, partly because of Christopher Columbus' claim to have discovered a route west to the Indies in 1492 (he had in fact found America). But in July 1497, an expedition of 170 men and four ships left Lisbon to open trading links between Portugal and India. It was led by Vasco da Gama.

▼ Map showing the journeys of Bartolomeu Dias (blue) and Vasco da Gama (red).

Having made a wide sweep out into the Atlantic to avoid the strong currents in the Gulf of Guinea, da Gama's ships rounded the Cape on 22nd November and sailed on up the east coast of Africa, soon passing the point reached by Dias nearly ten years earlier. By March, the expedition entered the waters along the coast where Muslims controlled the trade and from now on they discovered that many of the ports were inhabited by Arabs. As Christians, they encountered some hostility but in Malindi, just to the north of Mombasa, the ruler offered the services of an experienced Arab pilot, probably Ibn al-Majid, to guide them across the Indian Ocean.

At last, on 21st May 1498, da Gama and his ships anchored off the port of Calicut. The Indians were at first friendly but the Zamorin (sea-raja) of Calicut was unimpressed by the cheap trinkets the Portuguese hoped to exchange for the riches of the sub-continent. Da Gama's task was made still harder by Muslim merchants, anxious to protect their spice trade monopoly.

But when finally the Portuguese set sail on 29th August, they left with a valuable cargo of spices and precious stones. Da Gama also carried a letter from the Zamorin to King Manuel stating: 'In my kingdom there is an abundance of cinnamon, cloves, ginger, pepper and precious stones. What I seek from your country is gold, silver, coral and scarlet.' But most important of all, the Portuguese had found the direct sea route to the East and took back with them information on the vast potential of an unrestricted eastern trade.

▲ *Portrait of Vasco da Gama (1460-1524), the Portuguese captain who finally reached the coast of India.*

▼ *An engraving of the port of Calicut, on the western coast of India. It was here that the Portuguese made their first landing on Indian soil.*

chapter six

The European Trade Empires

The Open Door

▼ *A view of the Watch Tower in the Forbidden City, Beijing, built by the Ming rulers of China. The bronze statue of a dragon* (right) *is one of several inside the City.* ▶

▶ (far right) *A Hindu temple on the island of Bali, east of Java. Hinduism and later Islam were both introduced to Indonesia by Spice Route traders.*

The Portuguese found their new route to the East at an opportune moment. At the beginning of the Sixteenth Century, whilst many different nations were actively trading along the Spice Routes, there was no major naval power to block their way. The door for Portuguese expansion was wide open.

The Egyptians under the Mameluke empire were more concerned with defending their territories from the expansion of the Ottoman Turks; while the Turks, having won Egypt in 1517, were looking to advance into eastern Europe. In Iran, the Safavid Dynasty (1500-1629) was reviving that country's fortunes but it was essentially a land-based power, as were the kingdoms and sultanates of India.

Had the Portuguese arrived some seventy years earlier, the situation would have been very different, for then China was expanding its naval power. In 1368, the Yuan Dynasty had been toppled by the native Ming who were to control China for nearly three hundred years. The Ming Dynasty reached its peak during the reign of the third Ming emperor, Yung Lo (1403-24), who planned a huge programme of trade and exploration abroad. 27,000 men and a fleet of 317 ships were placed under the command of the admiral Zheng He (Cheng ho).

Between 1405 and 1433 Zheng He made seven great voyages. Amongst other places, he visited Thailand, Malaya, Java, Singapore, India, the Persian Gulf and the east coast of Africa. Part of his fleet may have even rounded the Cape of Good Hope – sixty years before Dias. But these expeditions halted abruptly in 1434. China was once again being attacked by the Mongols from the north and its shipping had begun to be harassed by Japanese pirates. The Chinese government therefore reverted to a defensive policy, breaking off all contacts with the West and no longer encouraging foreign trade.

It was unlikely, too, that the Portuguese would meet with much resistance in the Indonesian Archipelago. In the Thirteenth Century, this area had experienced a cultural golden age under the influence of the Majapahit Empire. A Hindu-Buddhist dynasty, with its capital in East Java, it had strong trading and political links through much of the Archipelago. But any unity had disintegrated in the Fourteenth Century and, with the arrival of Muslim traders, there was a gradual conversion to Islam. By 1511, when Portuguese ships first sailed into the area, there was a series of well-established but separate kingdoms ruled by Muslim sultans. Unsurprisingly, the wealth of these sultanates was built on their trade in spices.

▲ *This 14th Century bronze oil-lamp is in the style of the Majapahit Empire of East Java.*

A Portuguese
Empire in the East

Vasco da Gama returned to Portugal in 1499 with news of his breakthrough and the Portuguese were swift to follow this up. Increasing numbers of ships were sent round Africa to India and, in 1505, King Manuel sent a permanent force to India under the command of Francisco de Almeida. He was appointed the first Portuguese Viceroy (the king's representative) of India and set up his headquarters at Cochin on the Malabar Coast. Sri Lanka was next to be occupied in November of that year, giving the Portuguese access to its valuable cinnamon trees and a good strategic position on the Spice Route. In 1509 a combined Egyptian and Indian fleet was defeated by the Portuguese off the north coast of India. These successes established the Portuguese as serious competitors in the Indian Ocean trade, a position they were to maintain and expand on for over a century.

The Portuguese were never to succeed in completely breaking the Muslim hold on the Spice Routes. For example, even at the height of their strength, the amount of cloves they shipped to Europe via Africa was about 80 tons a year, whereas 1,300 tons of cloves, carried by Asian traders, reached Europe by the traditional routes through the Middle East. However, the Portuguese pursued a policy of capturing and holding major ports and demanding tolls or duties from any ships that used them. This gave them a vital stake in the Spice Route trade.

▲ *A church at Calangute, Goa, India built by the Portuguese. Soon after their arrival at Goa, the Portuguese set about converting the local people to Christianity.*

▶ *A Japanese lacquered screen of the Early Edo period (1573-1615). It shows the arrival of a Portuguese merchant ship at the port of Nagasaki.*

It was largely the actions of Alfonso de Albuquerque (1452-1515) that put Portugal in this position. In 1507, a force under his command seized Hormuz at the mouth of the Persian Gulf, so giving Portugal a commanding position on one of the main entry points of trade into the Middle East. In 1510, Albuquerque, now Viceroy of India, captured the rich port of Goa on the west coast of India. 'Golden Goa' soon replaced Calicut as India's leading trading port. Moving still further eastwards, Albuquerque seized Malaka in 1511. This port on the Straits of Malacca was one of the main distribution centres for Indonesian spices. As Tomé Pires, a Portuguese apothecary who lived in Malaka from 1512 to 1515, wrote, 'Whoever is lord of Malaka has his hands on the throat of Venice'. Indeed, one result of Portuguese expansion was Venice's loss of its monopoly of trade with the East. Other European cities, trading direct with the Portuguese, could now compete on an equal footing and Venice's power began to decline.

From their base at Malaka, the Portuguese were soon sailing direct to the Moluccas, China and Japan. Trade agreements with some of the Moluccas were established by 1513 and China was reached in 1515. The Chinese were less welcoming but eventually allowed the Portuguese to establish a trading post at Macao, close to Canton, in 1557. From here, the Portuguese could sail to Nagasaki in Japan. For the first time, Europeans were now actively trading along the whole length of the Spice Routes.

▲ *This carved stone bust forms part of the Viceroy's Arch in Goa, erected by the Portuguese in the early 16th Century.*

The Dutch Arrive

▼ *The frontispiece to a book that tells of the travels of one of the many Dutch East Indian traders.*

Portugal's trading empire was in effect a chain of different ports linked over great distances by the trade routes. Because it was so widely dispersed, the Portuguese had difficulty in providing the necessary supplies and finance to sustain it. Towards the end of the Sixteenth Century, the vulnerability of the Portuguese became increasingly obvious to other European nations. Two in particular, the Dutch and the English, were determined to become involved in direct trade with India and Southeast Asia or, as it was called, the East Indies.

In 1595, a group of Amsterdam merchants raised enough money to send out the first Dutch expedition to the East Indies. Its success prompted more ventures, each sponsored by rival groups of merchants. The competition between these groups was fierce so in 1602, to avoid a conflict of interests, the groups combined as the United East India Company (*Verenigde Oost-Indische Compagnie* or VOC for short). It had wide powers and was to become the driving force behind the Dutch colonial empire.

In 1603, a VOC expedition secured a valuable foothold for the Dutch on the Indian coast by making a treaty with the Zamorin of Calicut. Even more importantly, it then sailed on to the Moluccas where treaties of friendship were made with the rulers of Ternate and the Banda Islands. Crucially, in 1605, it captured the island of Amboyna from the Portuguese.

From this basis, the Dutch now set out to take complete control of the spice trade. With their larger numbers of soldiers and ships and superior weapons, they succeeded in driving the Portuguese from the Moluccas. They established their headquarters at the port of Batavia (Jakarta) on Java in 1619 and organized a blockade of Malaka (which the Portuguese finally surrendered in 1641). In 1656, they ousted the

▼ *A street scene in Batavia (Jakarta), Java, the Dutch capital of the East Indies.*

Portuguese from Sri Lanka. The Dutch were now Europe's most influential spice traders.

The Moluccas had welcomed the Dutch as liberators from the Portuguese but the Dutch concern for profits, which were often more than 1,000 per cent, was soon crippling the islanders. The Dutch prevented them from trading with anyone else and restricted the growth of certain spices to particular islands. To control production and prices in Europe, spices were burned or dumped in the sea, whilst nutmeg and clove trees were uprooted and destroyed. In 1625 alone, 65,000 clove trees were cut down in the Moluccas. Deprived of their main sources of income – spice cultivation and free trading – the people of the Moluccas were reduced to poverty and the splendid sultanates that had given the islands their name (Moluccas comes from the Arabic meaning 'the region of many kings') fell into decay.

▲ *Barbary pirates attack Dutch ships off the coast of North Africa. Ships frequently fell prey to pirates.*

▼ *An 18th Century porcelain figurine of a Dutch woman made in China for export to Europe.*

The English Challenge

▲ *An engraving of Drake's ship, the* Golden Hinde.

▶ *Portrait of Sir Francis Drake (c. 1545-96). In 1577 Drake embarked on his voyage round the world, returning to England in 1580.*

▼ *A Chinese porcelain plate of the 18th Century. The coat-of-arms of the British sovereign has been painted in the centre. The expansion of European trade led to a huge demand for Chinese porcelain and Chinese styles were considered highly fashionable.*

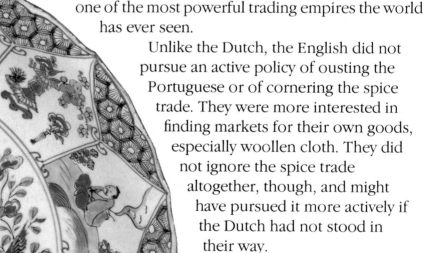

The Dutch were not without European rivals along the Spice Routes. Portuguese power did not disappear completely and English ships had already sailed in eastern seas before the arrival of the Dutch. In 1579, Francis Drake had reached the Moluccas during his famous journey around the world. His ship, the *Golden Hinde*, returned to England with a cargo of cloves, and the observations he made of the East Indies did much to fire the interest of contemporary English merchants. In 1600, the East India Company was founded in London – it was this threatened competition that led the Dutch merchants to unite under the VOC.

Funded by money from English merchants, the East India Company was granted a Royal Charter from Queen Elizabeth I. This gave the merchants of the company the authority to trade in the Far East for 15 years without interference from the Crown. Over the next 250 years, the East India Company was to grow into one of the most powerful trading empires the world has ever seen.

Unlike the Dutch, the English did not pursue an active policy of ousting the Portuguese or of cornering the spice trade. They were more interested in finding markets for their own goods, especially woollen cloth. They did not ignore the spice trade altogether, though, and might have pursued it more actively if the Dutch had not stood in their way.

ENGELANDT

The initial Company expeditions, leaving London in 1601 and 1604, had some success in trading with the Moluccas but thereafter the Dutch attacked the English wherever possible. In 1619, the two rivals entered a brief period of co-operation – the Dutch allowing the English a share of the spice trade in return for military assistance against the Portuguese – but this ended abruptly in 1623 when the Dutch sabotaged the agreement by murdering a number of English traders in Amboyna.

Over the next sixty years, the Dutch slowly but surely pushed the English out of the Moluccas' spice trade. The merchants of the English East India Company began to concentrate their attentions on the rich kingdoms of India. Here, the commercial opportunities were more open and – in the long term – more lucrative.

By the end of the Seventeenth Century the patterns of trade along the Spice Routes had changed dramatically. Prompted by the example of the Dutch and English, other European countries set up companies to trade with the East – amongst them were Belgium, Sweden, Denmark and notably France, who was to be England's main rival in India. With trade now flowing so freely round Africa, the Spice Routes of the Red Sea and the Persian Gulf were largely redundant. By 1713, Hormuz, once one of the Spice Routes' greatest ports, was virtually deserted. The proud Muslim empires of the Middle East were all but forgotten in the European scramble for power over east-west trade.

▲ *A 16th Century engraving of weavers at work. Woollen cloth was a major English export.*

▼ *Raffles' villa in western Sumatra. Sir Thomas Raffles (1781-1826) was an English colonial administrator who helped to increase British influence in the Far East. He founded Singapore in 1819 to rival Dutch-held Batavia.*

The Wealth of India

▲ *The stone gate towers of the Mughal fort at Lahore in Pakistan.*

▶ *Lengths of dyed cotton cloth dry in the sun on an Indian beach. Cotton has been a major industry in India for many centuries.*

Portrait of the Emperor Jahangir as a young man.

Lying at the heart of the Spice Routes, the Indian sub-continent had always played a vital role in their history. Traders from both East and West could meet in its ports to exchange their wares and, of course, purchase those that India produced itself. Indian goods, such as black pepper and cotton fabric, were in great demand in markets right across Asia and Europe, making a stop-over at one of India's ports not only convenient but highly profitable. By controlling some of these ports, European traders – firstly the Portuguese, then the Dutch, the French, the Danish and particularly the English – were able to take a sizeable share of the profits made on Indian trade.

That European control did not extend beyond this during the Sixteenth and Seventeenth Centuries was largely due to the power of the Mughal Empire. Claiming descent from the Mongols, the Mughals (from the Iranian word for Mongol) led by Babur had invaded India from Central Asia. By defeating the Sultan of Delhi in 1526, Babur had established Mughal rule in northern India and the empire continued to expand under his successors.

Foremost of these was the third emperor, Akbar (ruled 1556-1605). He was one of India's greatest rulers and his long reign is considered a golden age. He built a strong, centralized government run by both Muslims and Hindus (still the majority religion in India). Although himself a foreigner and a Muslim, he encouraged religious tolerance and the fusion of cultures this produced led to a flowering of science, art and literature. Magnificent buildings and monuments were erected and exquisite gardens laid out.

The Mughals also encouraged foreign trade. During the Sixteenth Century, the Portuguese, with their remarkable sailing skills, had found favour at the Mughal court and were allowed to trade freely along their north and eastern coasts. But when the Portuguese were defeated by the English at sea in 1611 the attitude of the court changed. In 1615, Akbar's son and successor, Jahangir (reigned 1605-27), received an official English ambassador at his court for the first time. The trade agreement that was negotiated then for the East India Company marked the beginning of England's increasing involvement with India.

Initially, England used its position of favour simply to build up trading activities through Asia, particularly with China. It was not until 1689 that the East India Company sought the support of the English Crown in establishing a 'nation of traders in India', that is to colonize the sub-continent, in order to give it a stronger grip on Asian trade. It was the decline of Mughal power in the early Eighteenth Century that gave the English the opportunity to fulfil this aim.

▼ *A miniature painting from a Mughal book* The Life of Akbar. *The great emperor Akbar receives the infant Prince Abdur Rahim at Agra Fort in 1562. The art of miniature painting flourished in India under Mughal rule.*

chapter seven

Changing Patterns of Trade

The Spice Routes Today

▲ *A ginger warehouse in the old Spice Route port of Cochin, where the spice trade still continues today.*

During the Eighteenth and Nineteenth Centuries, the major European powers increased their domination of the lands linked by the Spice Routes. At the start of this century the European colonial empires were at their peak: in Asia, the British held India, Sri Lanka, Burma, Thailand and the Malay Peninsula, the French Indo-China (Vietnam, Laos and Cambodia) and the Dutch most of the Indonesian Archipelago. The United States of America, a relatively new arrival on the Spice Routes, held the Philippines. But, by 1945, the financial impact of two world wars and the rise of Asian nationalism led to a rapid decline in western power. By 1947, India, Pakistan, Vietnam, Indonesia and the Philippines had gained their independence and the rest followed over the next twenty years. Today no one country can be said to dominate the Spice Routes.

No one country can be said to dominate the spice trade either. In about 1770, Pierre Poivre, a botanist and government official in the

French colony of Mauritius, succeeded in smuggling clove and nutmeg seedlings out of the Moluccas. By 1776 the first crop of cloves was successfully harvested on Mauritius. It was the beginning of the dispersal of spice cultivation to countries with suitable climates throughout the world. Prices began to drop and spices ceased to be among the most prized goods traded along the routes that bear their name. Today, spices are still grown in Indonesia, but they are of less importance in the Moluccas than crops such as rice and exotic fruits.

The Spice Routes still serve as highways for the transportation of goods between East and West. Many of the ports that grew up along their course still flourish, such as Foochow, Singapore, Cochin and Alexandria. But now other precious goods are carried along the Spice Routes in giant tankers and container ships: oil from the Middle East and motor cars and electrical goods from Japan. The age of the sail is long over and these huge ships now take a matter of weeks to travel from the Far East to Europe, a far cry from the many months the journey once took. Even swifter is the journey by aeroplane, while by computer, telephone and fax, it is possible to communicate with the other side of the world in a matter of seconds. Most of the countries along the Spice Routes are now easily accessible to the business traveller and, increasingly, the tourist.

Partly because of these vast improvements in communications, international trade now takes place on a scale and complexity that the early Spice Route merchants could never have dreamed of. Despite this, war and political upheaval still have the potential to change completely the patterns of trade, as recent events in China and the Middle East go to show. But, whatever happens, the Spice Routes will remain a major channel for cultural exchange between East and West.

▼ *A junk sails past the modern skyscrapers of Hong Kong, one of the world's major financial centres. Today, local trade along the Spice Routes is still carried out on traditional lines, in contrast to the international dealing in trade and commerce that takes place on the world's stock markets.*

45

A Spice Route Time Chart

Date	Europe	Middle East & Central Asia	China & the Far East
3000 BCE – 0	3000 *Minoan civilization, the earliest in Europe, develops in Crete.* c.1900 *Mycenaean civilization established on mainland Greece.* 753 *Traditional date for founding of Rome.* 336-323 *Empire of Alexander.* 146 *Greece comes under Roman rule.* 27 *End of Roman Republic. Octavian becomes Emperor.*	c.3000 *Egyptian hieroglyphics in use.* c.2000-1500 *Indus Valley civilization flourishes in what is now Pakistan.* c.1500-600 *Vedic Period in India, Hindu religion established.* 1000 *The Incense Road now in use.* c.500 *Buddhism founded in India.* 550-330 *The Persian Empire.* 247 *Parthians established in Iran.* 30 *Egypt made a Roman province.*	c.2205-1766 *Xia dynasty in China* c.1766-1027 *Shang dynasty in China.* 1027-221 *Zhou dynasty in China.* 660 *Legendary date for founding of Japan under Emperor Jimmu.* 202 *Han dynasty takes over China.* 150 BCE-50 CE *Dong-son culture in North Vietnam.* c.100 *Silk Route fully open from China to the West.*
1 CE – 500	117 CE *Roman Empire at its largest.* c.200 *Barbarians begin attacking frontiers of Roman Empire.* 330 *Constantinople established as new capital of the Roman Empire.* 395 *Roman Empire splits into two.* 476 *Western Roman Empire collapses.* 486 *Frankish kingdom formed, with land in Germany and France.*	c.29 CE *Death of Jesus Christ. Spread of Christianity begins.* 224 *Sasanians oust Parthians and establish empire through western Asia.* c.250 *Sasanians control much of spice trade.* 320 *Gupta Empire founded in India.*	73-91 CE *Chinese defeat Xiongnu in Tarim region.* 220 *Han dynasty collapses. China breaks into three.* c.300 *Yamato government established in Japan.* 316 *Japan invades Korea.* 316-598 *Rival dynasties in north and south China.*
501 – 1000	610 *Roman Empire now focused around eastern Mediterranean; known as Byzantine Empire.* 711 *Arabs conquer Spain.* 732 *Arab advance into Europe halted at Battle of Poitiers.* 768-814 *Charlemagne reigns over the Franks.* 793-94 *Vikings begin raiding northern Europe.*	535 *Gupta Empire collapses.* 632 *Death of Muhammad. Muslim Arab expansion begins.* 651 *Muslims control Mesopotamia and Iran, and East-West trade.* 661-750 *Umayyad dynasty rules Muslim Empire from Damascus.* 750-1258 *Abbasid dynasty rules from Baghdad.* mid-900s *Muslim Empire fragments.*	552 *Buddhism introduced into Japan.* 581 *Yang Chien founds the Sui dynasty. He unites China in 589.* 618-907 *Tang dynasty rules in China.* 794-1185 *Heian Period in Japan.* 802-1431 *Kingdom of Angkor in Cambodia under Khmer dynasty.* 907-76 *End of Tang dynasty. China divided by civil wars.* 976 *Sung dynasty reunites China.*
1001 – 1500	c.1001 *Start of Medieval period.* 1204 *Fourth Crusade, led by the Venetians, sacks Constantinople.* 1236 *Mongols invade Russia.* 1271 *Marco Polo sets out for the East.* 1348 *Black Death ravages Europe.* c.1400 *Renaissance period begins.* 1453 *Byzantine Empire collapses.* 1488 *Bartolomeu Dias sails round the Cape of Good Hope.* 1497-99 *Vasco da Gama's journey.*	1096 *First Crusade. Christian crusaders capture Jerusalem.* 1187 *Muslims regain Jerusalem.* 1260-1368 *Mongols control Central Asia. Overland trade prospers.* 1281-1326 *Reign of Osman I, founder of Turkish Ottoman Empire.* 1325 *Ibn Battuta's travels begin.* 1405 *Final collapse of Mongol power. Spice Routes now remain only effective channel for East-West trade.*	1126 *China divided into two.* 1156-85 *Civil wars in Japan.* 1196 *Ghengis Khan unites Mongols.* 1264 *Mongol (Yuan) dynasty founded in China.* 1368 *Yuan dynasty overthrown and replaced by Chinese Ming dynasty.* 1405-33 *Chinese explore Spice Routes.* c.1450 *China adopts isolationist foreign policy.* 1477-1568 *Provincial wars in Japan.*
1501 – 1700	1521 *Silk manufacture begins in France.* 1529 *Turks besiege Vienna.* 1571 *Battle of Lepanto; Turks are defeated by Spanish and Venetians. Marks end of Turkish sea power in Mediterranean.* 1600 *English East India Company founded.* 1602 *Dutch United East India Company (VOC) founded.* 1652-74 *Anglo-Dutch Trade Wars.* 1689-1725 *Reign of Peter the Great of Russia. Russia becomes a major European power.*	1502 *Safavid dynasty established in Iran.* 1510 *Portuguese capture Goa.* 1526 *Mughals defeat Sultan of Delhi and are established in India.* 1556-1605 *Reign of third Mughal Emperor, Akbar the Great.* 1566 *Ottoman Empire at its largest.* 1594 *English begin trading in India.* 1605-27 *Reign of Mughal Emperor Jahangir.* 1611 *English East India Company establishes a trading post in India.* 1696 *English establish a trading base at Calcutta.*	1511 *Portuguese take Malaka.* 1514 *Portuguese reach China.* 1521 *Portuguese reach Moluccas.* 1570 *Nagasaki, Japan, opened to foreign traders.* 1596 *Dutch in East Indies.* 1619 *Dutch establish headquarters at Batavia (Jakarta) in Java.* 1623 *Amboyna Massacre. Dutch destroy English base in East Indies.* 1637 *Foreigners forbidden in Japan.* 1641 *Dutch sieze Malaka.* 1644 *Chinese Ming dynasty ends. Qing (Manzhou) dynasty founded.* 1685 *China open to foreign trade.*

Glossary

Buddhism: a religious path taught in India by Siddhartha Gautama (c.560-486BCE), known as the Buddha. It declares that by understanding the origins of all human suffering, people can reach perfect enlightenment or *nirvana*.

Byzantium: the original name for Constantinople (now Istanbul), the capital of the Eastern Roman Empire. The empire became known as the Byzantine Empire (610-1453CE) and is often simply referred to as Byzantium.

Chola Coast: the ancient name given to the eastern coast of India, now also known as the Coromandel Coast. Important ports grew up along the coast from the trade with the Far East.

Christianity: the religion founded in Palestine by the followers of Jesus of Nazareth (c.5BCE-29CE), later known as Jesus Christ. His teachings spread rapidly through the Roman Empire until Christianity became the official state religion towards the end of the 4th Century CE.

Christopher Columbus: Italian navigator (1451-1506). In the service of Spain, he discovered America, the New World, in 1492. He believed, however, that he had reached the Far East and, for as long as he lived, never realized the significance of his discovery.

colonize: to establish a colony in an area. A colony is a settlement of people in a distant country who maintain close ties with their homeland. A colonial empire is subject territory occupied by settlement from the ruling state.

dhow: an Arab ship of varying size with one or two masts and a lateen (triangular) sail, which enabled the ship to sail forwards even when the wind blew from the side. Dhows are still used by some Arab sailors today.

Hinduism: a religion established in India during the Vedic Period (c.1500-600BCE). It is characterized by the worship of many gods, including Brahma as the supreme being, and the belief in reincarnation.

Huns: see *Xiongnu*.

incense: once very rare and costly, it is made from various sweet-smelling substances, usually the sap from certain plants and trees. Crystals of the dried sap are sprinkled on to hot coals and they produce a perfumed smoke. Spices and fragrant woods are also sometimes burnt as incense.

Islam: this means literally 'surrender' (to God). Islam is a religion founded by Muhammad (c.570-632CE) whose followers became known as Muslims. The *Qur'an* is Islam's sacred scripture which teaches that there is only one God and that Muhammad is His prophet.

Malabar Coast: the south-western coast of India. A string of ports grew up from the trade with the Middle East and Europe. Black pepper was one of the most important products of the region.

Marco Polo: a Venetian merchant (1254-1324), famous for his account of his travels in Asia. After travelling overland to China (1271-75) with his father and uncle, he spent 17 years serving the Mongol emperor of China, Kublai Khan, before returning to Venice by sea (1292-95).

Mecca: located in western Saudi Arabia. It was where the founder of Islam, Muhammad, was born. It is the holiest city of Islam and is a centre of pilgrimage for Muslims, who come to worship at the Kaaba, a sacred black stone inside the mosque.

Mesopotamia: means 'between the rivers'. It is the name given by the Ancient Greeks to the region between the Tigris and Euphrates rivers, now in modern Iraq. The earliest civilizations grew up in this fertile area.

Mongols: various nomadic tribes from the part of the Steppes now called Mongolia. In 1206 they were united by Temujin (c.1162-1227), who overpowered the other Mongol tribes and became Ghengis Khan (supreme ruler). He and his sons and grandsons conquered one of the largest empires in history.

monopoly: the exclusive control over the supply of a product or service. For example, the complete control of the trade in spices by one organization.

monsoon: this is the seasonal wind of southern Asia that blows from the south-west during the summer months, bringing heavy rains, and from the north-east during the winter.

Muslim: see *Islam*.

nationalism: a feeling based on common cultural characteristics that binds a population. It often produces a desire for independence or separation. Nationalism can also describe devotion (often fanatical) to one's country.

Parthians: a tribe from the area south-east of the Caspian Sea in Asia. They controlled a great empire dominating western Asia from the 2nd Century BCE. Weakened by internal feuds and attacks from Roman armies, the Parthian Empire fell to the Sasanians in 224 CE.

Persia: the name given, until 1935, to Iran. Today, it usually describes the ancient Persian Empire, that lasted for over 200 years from 550 BCE until 330 BCE.

Phoenicians: an ancient people of skilled sailors and great merchants. From about 1100 BCE they lived in cities such as Sidon and Tyre along the eastern coast of the Mediterranean Sea in the area now known as the Lebanon.

pilot: in shipping terms, a person who acts as a guide or navigator on board a ship bound for a particular port or navigating coastal waters.

porcelain: a very fine ceramic material used to make plates. The Chinese developed the technique of making porcelain by 900 CE.

Sasanians: the ruling people of Iran from 224 CE, after their defeat of the Parthians. Over the next 400 years, until they in turn fell before the might of Islam in 642 CE, the Sasanians controlled much of the territory in western Asia that had been part of the great Persian Empire.

silk: the very fine fibre produced by silk worms when they make their cocoons. Threads of silk are made from the fibres and these can be woven together to make fabrics. The craft of producing silk and its cloth its known as sericulture.

Tomé Pires: Portuguese writer, pharmacist and accountant who worked at the trading station at Malaka. He wrote a book called *Suma Oriental* ('Sum of the East') about trade on the Malabar Coast, Malaysia, Java and Sumatra. Later, in 1521, he travelled as an envoy to China where he died in captivity in about 1540.

Turks: natives of Turkey, but the name is also applied to Turkic speaking people as a whole. The Turks originated in Central Asia but pushed westwards into Byzantine territories during the 15th Century. They established their own empire, known as the Ottoman Empire (after the ruling Ottoman dynasty) through the Middle East and Balkan region of Europe.

Xiongnu: a nomadic people who originated from the Steppe region of northern Central Asia. They are thought to be the same people Europe knew as the Huns. From the 3rd Century BCE onwards, the warrior horsemen periodically terrorized the Chinese and the kingdoms of Central Asia. In the 4th and 5th Centuries CE, the Xiongnu/Huns ventured as far west as Europe and their attacks were partly responsible for the decline of Roman power.

Index

First published in Great Britain in 1993 by
Belitha Press Limited
31 Newington Green, London N16 9PU

Reprinted 1994

Copyright text © Belitha Press Limited/UNESCO 1993
Illustration/photographs copyright © in this format by Belitha Press Limited/UNESCO 1993

ISBN 1 85561 161 9
ISBN 92 3 102762 X (UNESCO)

Typeset by Chambers Wallace, London
Printed in Spain for Imago

British Library Cataloguing in Publication Data for this book is available from the British Library.

Editor: Rachel Cooke
Designer: John Calvert
Series Consultant: Dr André Singer
Specialist Consultants: Dr Peter Carey and Amiral Bellec
Maps by Swanston Graphics Ltd, David Gifford and
   Eugene Fleury.

Acknowledgements

The Ancient Art and Architecture Collection 6 top left, 20 top left; Aspect Picture Library 20/21, 26 top left, 27 bottom right, 29 bottom right, 34; Bibliothèque Nationale cover, 17 bottom, 24; British Library 15 bottom left, 38 bottom left, 41 bottom, 42 bottom left; British Museum 12 top left; Christie's Colour Library 35 top right, 39 bottom right, 40 bottom left; The Cleveland Museum of Art, Leonard C Hanna, Jr. Fund 60.194 36, 37; © Comstock Inc/David Beatty/Susan Griggs 44 top left; © Comstock Inc/Nik Wheeler/Susan Griggs 44/45; E T Archive 9 top right, 18 centre, 23 centre right, 27 top left, 29 centre left, 39 top; Mary Evans Picture Library 6 bottom left, 11 top right and left, bottom left, 30, 31, 32/33, 38 top left, 40 top left and centre; Sally & Richard Greenhill 8 bottom right; Robert Harding Picture Library 28 top left, 29 top right, 33 top right, 42 top left; Michael Holford 8 top left, 9 bottom right, 18 bottom left, 30 top left; The Hutchison Library 26 bottom; The Image Bank 35 bottom; Magnum/Abbas 7 bottom; Magnum/Barbey 15 bottom right, 25 top right; Magnum/Mayer 17 top right; The Mansell Collection 11 bottom right, 12 right, 13 bottom, 16, 28 bottom left, 31 top right; Cultural Relics Bureau, Beijing & Metropolitan Museum of Art 12 bottom; Toby Molenaar 42 right; Christine Osborne Pictures 37 right; Österreichische Nationalbibliothek 19 bottom right; Picturepoint 7 top right, 14 top left, 36 top left; Ann Ronan Picture Library 41 top right; Royal Botanic Gardens, Kew 10 top and bottom left, and bottom centre; South Africa Tourist Board 32 top left; Topkapi Palace Museum 25 top right; UNESCO/Earl Kowall/Silk Roads Photograph donated by the photographer to the 'Integral Study of the Silk Roads: Roads of Dialogue' 23 top; Victoria and Albert Museum 21 top right, 43.